TOTALLY TOP SECRET

by Jake Black

PSS!
PRICE STERN SLOAN
An Imprint of Penguin Group (USA) LLC

QUIZ + ACTIVITY BOOK

PRICE STERN SLOAN
Published by the Penguin Group
Penguin Group (USA) LLC, 375 Hudson Street, New York, New York 10014, USA

USA | Canada | UK | Ireland | Australia | New Zealand | India | South Africa | China

penguin.com
A Penguin Random House Company

Published in 2014 by Price Stern Sloan, a division of Penguin Young Readers Group, 345 Hudson Street, New York, New York 10014. *PSS!* is a registered trademark of Penguin Group (USA) LLC. Printed in the USA.

ISBN 978-0-8431-8247-7   10 9 8 7 6 5 4

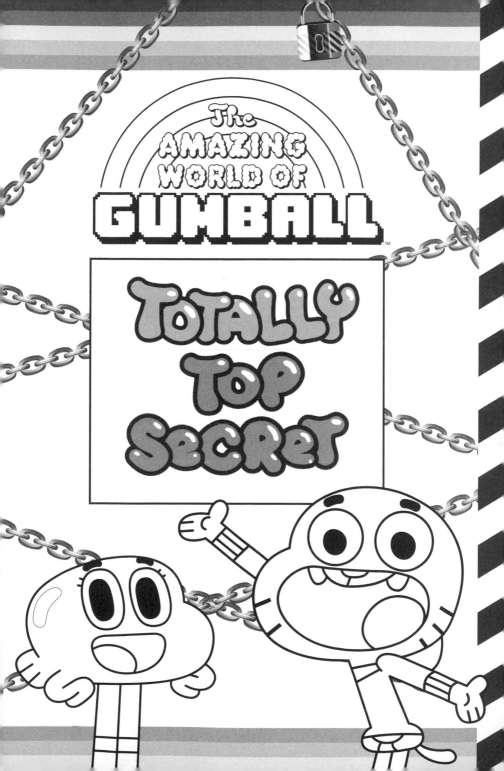

CONTENTS

Welcome 6-7

Crack the Code 8-9

Maze 10

Word Search 11

Search and Find 12-13

Crossword 14

Door Hangers 15-18

Crack the Code 19

Pop Quiz 20-21

Jokes 22-24

Maze 25

Guess Who? 26

Connect the Dots 27

New Student 28-29

Scrambled Names 30

Matching 31

Spot the Difference 32

In the Shadows 33

Memory Quiz 34-36

Soccer Word Search 37

Comic 38-39

Game 40-41

Color Us Cool 42

Guess Who? 43

Family Time 44-45

Search and Find 46-47

Party Planner 48-49

Anais's Diary 50-51

Spot the Differences 52-53

Map It Out 54-55

Art Class 56-57

The Missing Piece 58

Squares 59

Connect the Dots 60

Answers 61-64

Hey, everybody! I'm so glad you decided to come and play! This book is full of all sorts of way awesome games, puzzles, jokes, and riddles! You'll love it! It's about my friends and me, and the wild stuff we do at school.

SOME OF THESE
ACTIVITIES YOU CAN
DO WITH YOUR FRIENDS.
OTHERS YOU DO BY
YOURSELF. GIVE THEM
YOUR BEST SHOT. I'M
SURE YOU'LL HAVE TONS
OF FUN! AND JUST
SO YOU KNOW, THE
ANSWERS ARE IN THE
BACK OF THE BOOK.

SO, WHAT ARE YOU
WAITING FOR? GRAB
A PENCIL AND GET
PLAYIN'!

oh yeah!!

I, GUMBALL, HAVE WRITTEN A SECRET LETTER TO MY ONE TRUE LOVE, PENNY. USE THE CODE BELOW TO FIND OUT JUST HOW I FEEL ABOUT MY SUPER CRUSH.

Alphabet minus 1 to the left.

A-B-C-D-E-F-G-H-I-J-
K-L-M-N-O-P-Q-R-S-
T-U-V-W-X-Y-Z

Done

Efbs qfooz,
IPx EP J mPWf zPv, mfu
Nf dpvou uif xbzt:
zPvs dvuf boumfst, zPvs
bEpsbcmf wpjdf, zPvs psbohf
tofblfst. zPv'sf bo bxftPNf
diffsmfbEfs, boE zPv spdl
tzodispojaFE txjNNjoh. J
xjmm bmxbzt mPWf zPv.
Nz ifbsu cfmpoht up zPv,
HvNcbmm

HAZE

Uh-oh. We didn't listen to Miss Simian, and now we're lost in the Forest of Doom. Can you help us find our way back to Miss Simian and our classmates before the picnic is over?

FINISH

START

WORD SEARCH

Hey, you're smart! Help us find these special words hidden on the page.

Elmore
Miss Simian
Granny JoJo
Laser Video
Tina Rex

Joyful Burger
Carmen
Daisy
The Eggheads
Hot Dog Guy

R D H P D B W J T T L T H M F
G Z T O T Q S Q X D N N V I W
R B E F E H P Q T Z V N C S Y
R S P O X D E I Y C O S A S U
A M B P K H I E W Q D D R S G
T I N A R E X V G L P M M I G
J O Y F U L B U R G E R E M O
E S G C J S F M X E H Q N I D
J L Q Y F S O J M L S E W A T
E A M F Q B I V J D D A A N O
N O J O J Y N N A R G G L D H
M A J M R V B I J G L V J J S
T Y D X U E S A J C X Z W V L
O Z H W A Y J V F I Y E L E Z

SEARCH AND FIND

Darn! I've lost a couple things at school. Can you help me find them?

My friend Banana Joe
My school book
My family's remote control
a hot dog
a pizza
a box of Daisy Flakes

Bet you can help us do this crossword puzzle!

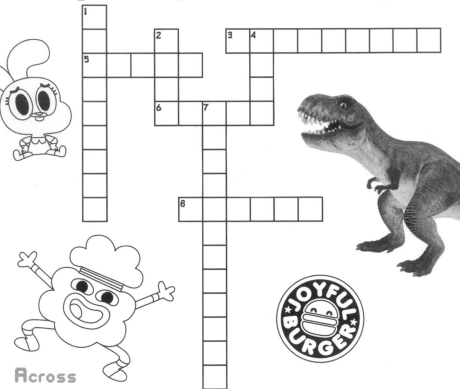

Across

3. Name of the fast-food restaurant in Elmore

5. Gumball's little sister

6. A crumbly piece of toast

8. The Jock at Elmore Junior High School

Down

1. An office building in Elmore

2. Elmore Junior High School's dinosaur

4. The balloon who loves Carmen

7. The Wattersons' next-door neighbors

DOOR HANGERS

Make your very own totally cool Gumball door hangers! Ask an adult to help cut out the pieces and then color them in!

STAY OUT OF MY ROOM, DUDE!

C'MON IN AND JOIN THE PARTY!

QUIET!

GENIUSNESS

GOING

ON

INSIDE!

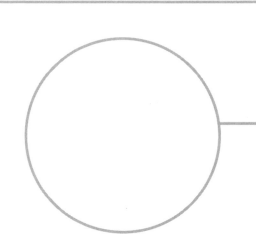

PUMP UP
THE VOLUME!

Anais thinks that no one in the family knows about her diary. Well, she's wrong! Help me and Darwin figure out what she's written using the secret code below.

!daeh reh fo kcab eht

ni seye sah ehS .moM htiw

yrots tnereffid a s'ti tub

,emit eht fo tsom daD loof

nac yehT .eucser rieht ot

gnimoc pu dne syawla I

dna ,elbuort otni gnitteg

era syawla yehT .semitemos

yzarc em evird yeht tub

,srehtorb ym evol I

Hint: Backward text and bottom to top reading

So, you think you know me, my family and friends, and the town of Elmore? Take this pop quiz to find out!

Where does Gumball's mom, Nicole Watterson, work?

_____

Which person works at the convenience store, the gas station, and the DVD shop in Elmore?

_____

What's the name of the pizzeria in Elmore?

_____

What's the name of the school counselor at Elmore Junior High school?

_____

Miss Simian has been teaching second grade for how many years?

_____

What's the name of the foreign exchange student at Elmore Junior High school?

_____

What's the name of Anais's stuffed donkey?

_____

What's the population of Elmore?

_____

What's the name of the highway that goes through Elmore?

_____

How old is Anais?

_____

✿ **8-10** correct: You're awesome, dude!

✿ **5-7** correct: You're gonna have to do more homework.

✿ **Fewer than 5** correct: Detention!

WHAT DO YOU DO IF MISS SIMIAN ROLLS HER EYES AT YOU?

PICK THEM UP AND ROLL THEM BACK TO HER!

MOM, I JUST KNOCKED OVER THE LADDER IN THE BACKYARD!

WELL, TELL YOUR DAD.

HE KNOWS. HE'S HANGING FROM THE ROOF.

WHY DID PRINCIPAL BROWN GO OUT WITH A PRUNE?

BECAUSE HE COULDN'T FIND A DATE.

WHAT DO YOU CALL A PIG THAT KNOWS KARATE? A PORK CHOP!

HEY, WE KNOW KARATE! DOES THAT MAKE US A CAT CHOP AND A FISH CHOP?

Dad has an interview at Chanax Inc. Can you please help him find his way there?

START

FINISH

Use the clues to guess who this Elmore Junior High School student is. Write your answer in the space at the bottom of the page.

I live in the junkyard.

I am very large.

I have a long tail, powerful legs, and short arms.

I can be a little bit mean sometimes.

I'm a dinosaur.

_____

Gumball has a brother who used to be his pet goldfish. Connect the dots to reveal who this pet-turned-sibling actually is!

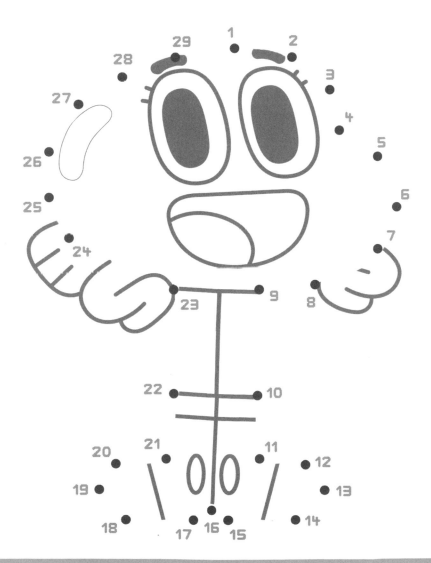

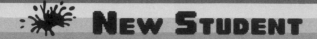

NEW STUDENT

Welcome to Elmore Junior High School! As a new student, you'll need to get registered. You can do this by answering the questions below. In the space provided on the next page, draw a self portrait that we'll use for your brand-new Elmore Junior High School student ID.

Name: _____

Where Do You Live?: _____

Favorite Food: _____

Favorite Movie: _____

Favorite Subject in School: _____

Favorite After-School Activity: _____

Favorite Music: _____

Favorite TV Show: _____

Favorite Book: _____

Favorite Type of Pet: _____

Hair Color: _____

Eye Color: _____

What Style of Clothes Do You Like to Wear?:

_____

SCRAMBLED NAMES

Can you unscramble the words below? Write your answers in the spaces provided.

Lglbmau _____

TaNi _____

ENpyN _____

CraEhl _____

AmcNEr _____

RdaNiW _____

ObrbEt _____

Draw a line from each character to his or her parent.

1. Gumball

2. Tobias

3. Rocky

4. Penny

5. Tina

a. Gaylord

B. Mr. Rex

C. Richard

D. Mr. Fitzgerald

E. Harold

Look closely at the four pictures below. One of them is different. Which one is it?

Can you identify the characters below?

_____ _____

_____ _____

_____ _____

Study the picture on these two pages very carefully and memorize as many details as you can.

Then turn the page and answer the questions from memory. Remember, no peeking!

1. Where did this picture happen?

_____

_____

2. How many characters are in the picture?

_____

_____

3. Is Gumball happy or sad?

_____

_____

4. What is everybody doing? (For example, playing a game? Sitting in class? Eating lunch?)

_____

_____

5. How many windows are in the background?

_____

_____

6. Who are the grown-ups in the picture?

_____

_____

SOCCER WORD SEARCH

Gumball loves playing soccer. Find the soccer terms listed below in the word search.

Soccer
Kick
Goalie
Winners

Points
Cleats
Jersey
Head

Yellow Card
Field

T	S	G	P	V	G	B	K	G	H	A	Y	P	P	H
Y	E	L	L	O	W	C	A	R	D	H	Q	N	N	D
E	N	R	A	T	I	U	S	X	C	X	H	U	R	P
S	B	L	D	K	N	N	X	F	K	V	B	P	A	U
R	I	X	Y	T	N	D	T	P	U	P	U	R	B	J
E	A	N	C	L	E	A	T	S	H	Z	S	J	G	R
J	H	Y	V	G	R	E	Q	S	K	I	J	V	F	Q
O	G	F	V	N	S	H	B	D	L	A	Y	P	Z	R
C	U	P	P	J	O	D	N	G	K	H	F	O	L	P
N	K	Y	D	H	C	B	E	V	N	A	Q	R	G	A
F	L	P	J	L	C	H	D	G	O	S	A	G	W	Z
V	D	K	D	H	E	B	F	G	U	J	U	C	P	J
X	X	C	H	G	R	I	S	J	Q	Y	P	G	R	U
H	M	E	D	G	X	I	F	R	Q	B	I	T	T	C

 **COMIC**

Make your own *The Amazing World of Gumball* comic by adding words and pictures to each panel.

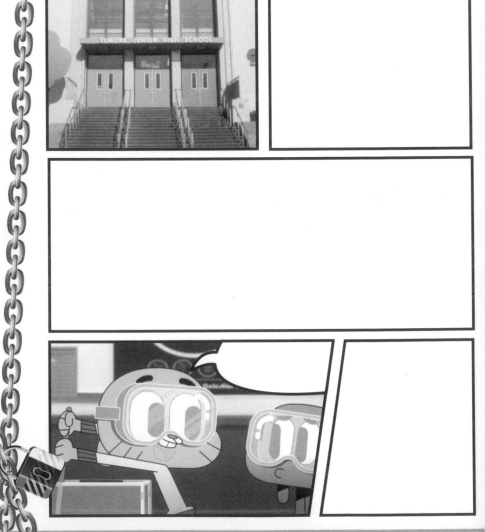

GAME

School can be a crazy place, filled with adventures, challenges, and lots of learning—of course. Play this game with a friend, using pennies as game pieces. Place your pennies at the Elmore Junior High School starting space and take turns moving around the game board. On your turn, flip a coin—move ahead two spaces for heads, one space for tails. The first player to make it to Gumball's house wins.

Got an "A" on your homework. **JUMP AHEAD ONE SPACE.**

START

Forgot your locker combination. **GO BACK ONE SPACE.**

FIN FLAPPIN' TASTIC

oh yeah!!

FINISH

You made it!
You are the best
student at
Elmore Junior
High School!
YOU WIN!

BUS STOP

Missed the
bus home.
**GO BACK
THREE
SPACES.**

Elected
student-body
president.
**JUMP
AHEAD TWO
SPACES.**

What the What?

CHOCOLATE DRINK

Got your
favorite food
at lunch!
**JUMP AHEAD
ONE SPACE.**

You won
the soccer
game. **JUMP
AHEAD ONE
SPACE.**

Tina and her
friends chased
you down the
hall. **GO BACK
ONE SPACE.**

COLOR US COOL

Use crayons, colored pencils, markers, paint, or whatever to color in the picture below!

Use the clues to guess who this Elmore Junior High School student is. Write your answer in the space at the bottom of the page.

People call me the smartest student at Elmore Junior High School.

I do not have emotions.

I have different "modes" for different situations.

My best friend is Ocho.

I am a robot.

_____

FAMILY TIME

There are families of all types in Elmore, USA. Big ones and small ones, but the most important thing is that they all love each other. Draw a picture of your family in the space provided and tell us about them.

SEARCH AND FIND

Find and circle the following objects in the picture:

Daisy the DONKEY doll
a paper airplane
a toaster
a boom box
a paper bag
a fish bowl
Bobert
Leslie
a die

🤘 PARTY PLANNER

It's the end of the school year! Let's throw a party! First, we've got to plan the party so it can be the biggest, best party in the history of parties.

Date: _____

Where: _____

Who do you want to invite?

_____

_____

What's the theme (for example, pirates, the '80s, etc.)?

_____

What's on the menu?

_____

_____

What games should we play?

_____

_____

_____

What music should we blast?

_____

_____

_____

How should we decorate?

_____

_____

_____

DODGE
OR
DARE

J U N I O R H I G H
P A R T Y

ANAIS'S DIARY

Anais loves writing in her diary. You can write in your own diary, too, by answering the questions below.

Today at school I:

That made me feel:

After school I:

I liked that because:

I didn't like it because:

at home I like to:

My parents and I talked about:

for dinner I ate:

Compare these two pictures of Elmore Junior High School. Eight things have been changed. Can you find all eight?

_____   _____

_____   _____

_____   _____

_____   _____

MAP IT OUT

Elmore, USA, is a great place to live, work, and go to school! Put your knowledge of the town to the test by following these instructions.

1. Put an *X* on the place where everyone goes to school.

2. Circle the place where you can play soccer.

3. Draw a triangle around Gumball's house.

4. Draw a line from Gumball's house to where his mom works.

5. Put a square around the place you go if you get sick.

6. Draw some trees in the forest.

7. Make up and write a new name for the Rainbow Factory.

_____

8. Put a star on your favorite store.

9. Color a rainbow at the Rainbow Factory.

In art class, we're learning how to draw a picture using a grid. Check out the picture in the grid below and then copy it square by square in the empty grid on the next page.

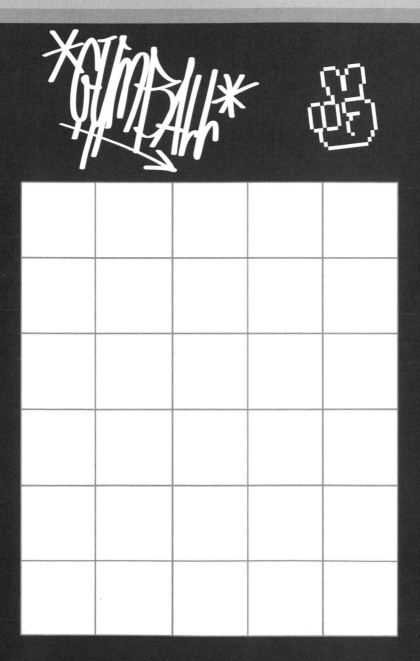

THE MISSING PIECE

Which piece is missing from the puzzle? Look closely, then circle it.

SQUARES

During Halloween, Gumball called Darwin a square because he was a little bit scared. In this game, you make squares—but not because they're scared. Play this game with a friend. Each player takes a turn connecting two dots, one line at a time, to make a square. The lines should only be horizontal and vertical, not diagonal. When you complete the square, put your initial in it and circle the square. Then, take another turn. You can use your opponent's lines to make squares. The player with the most squares wins.

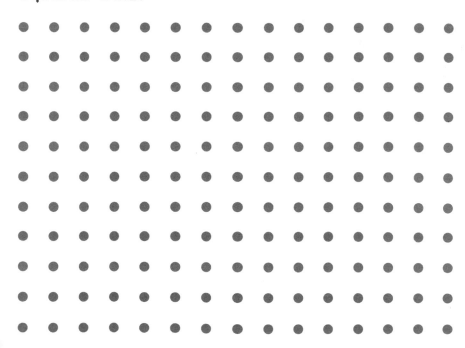

My teacher at school has been teaching since the Stone Age. That's, like, forever. Connect the dots to reveal her identity.

8-9: Crack the Code

Dear Penny,
How do I love you, let me count the ways:
Your cute antlers, your adorable voice, your orange sneakers. You're an awesome cheerleader, and you rock synchronized swimming. I will always love you.
My heart belongs to you,
Gumball

10: Maze

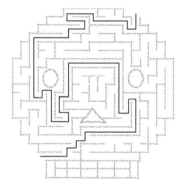

11: Word Search

12-13: Search and Find

14: Crossword

1: CHANAX INC
2: TINA
3: LAZY LARRY
4: ALAN
5: ANAIS
6: ANTON
7: THE ROBINSONS
8: TOBIAS

19: Crack the Code

I love my brothers, but they drive me crazy sometimes. They always are getting into trouble, and I always end up coming to their rescue. They can fool Dad most of the time, but it's a different story with Mom. She has eyes in the back of her head!

20-21: Pop Quiz

The Rainbow Factory
Laurence "Larry"
    Needlemeyer
Fervidus Pizza
Mr. Steve Small
300,000

Juke
Daisy the Donkey
20,000
Elmore Expressway
4 years old

25: Maze

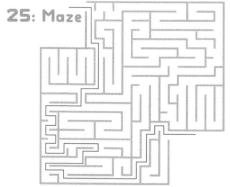

26: Guess Who?

Tina Rex

27: Connect the Dots

30: Scrambled Names

Gumball
Tina
Penny
Rachel
Carmen
Darwin
Bobert

31: Matching

1. Gumball — D. Mr. Fitzgerald
2. Tobias — E. Harold
3. Rocky — B. Mr. Rex
4. Penny — C. Richard
5. Tina — a. Gaylord

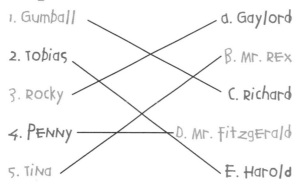

32: Spot the Difference

33: In the Shadows

Carmen
Ocho
Gumball
Leslie
Idaho
Banana Joe

36: Memory Quiz

1. school yard
2. three
3. happy
4. Gumball & Darwin looking at Bobert
5. four
6. None

43: Guess Who?

Bobert

46-47: Search and Find

58: The Missing Piece

37: Soccer Word Search

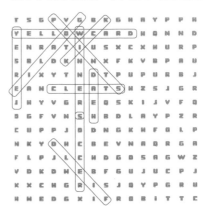

52: Spot the Differences

60: Connect the Dots